Blue Line 2

Vokabellernheft

Herausgeber: Dr. Frank Haß

Ernst Klett Verlag
Stuttgart • Leipzig

Liebe Schülerin, lieber Schüler,

mit diesem Vokabellernheft im praktischen Taschenformat kannst du überall deine Wörter lernen, wiederholen und nachschlagen.
In den Wortlisten kannst du Wörter und Wendungen, die dir schwierig vorkommen, mit Textmarker oder Bleistift markieren, um sie dann immer wieder durchzugehen.
Auch die vielen Übungen nach jeder Unit unterstützen dich bei der Wiederholung. So kannst du dich prima auf Vokabeltests vorbereiten.

In den Übungen, die mit diesem Zeichen ● gekennzeichnet sind, übst du die blau gedruckten Wörter.

Hinter jedem Wort ist die Lautschrift (z. B. [fæn'tæstɪk] für *fantastic*) angegeben. Diese hilft dir, wenn du nicht weißt, wie du das Wort aussprechen sollst.
Hilfreiche Hinweise zum Umgang mit den Lautschriftzeichen findest du **in deinem Englischbuch** auf Seite 187 und ab Seite 236 am unteren Rand aller *Dictionary*-Seiten.

Viel Erfolg beim Vokabellernen!

Unit 1 Friends

Way in

p. 8	**I'm fine.** [ˌaɪm 'faɪn]	Mir geht es gut.
	late [leɪt]	(zu) spät
p. 9	**Jamaica** [dʒə'meɪkə]	Jamaika
	holiday ['hɒlədeɪ]	Ferien; Urlaub
	fantastic [fæn'tæstɪk]	fantastisch; großartig
	to **visit** ['vɪzɪt]	besuchen
	grandparents *(pl)* ['grænˌpeərənts]	Großeltern
	scarf *(sg)* [skɑ:f], **scarves** *(pl)* [skɑ:vz]	Schal; Tuch
p. 8	to **ask about** ['ɑ:sk‿əˌbaʊt]	sich erkundigen nach; fragen nach
	to **talk about** ['tɔ:k‿əˌbaʊt]	sprechen über
	to **have to** ['hæv tə], **had to** ['hæd tə]	müssen
	uncle ['ʌŋkl]	Onkel
p. 9	**hat** [hæt]	Hut

Station 1

Holiday activities

to **start a band** [ˌstɑ:t‿ə 'bænd]	eine Band gründen
to **go shopping** [ˌgəʊ 'ʃɒpɪŋ]	einkaufen gehen
to **stay in a hotel** [ˌsteɪ ɪn‿ə həʊ'tel]	in einem Hotel übernachten
to **pack a suitcase** [ˌpæk‿ə 'su:tkeɪs]	einen Koffer packen
to **hang (around)** [hæŋ], **hung** [hʌŋ]	(herum)hängen

to climb a mountain [ˌklaɪm‿ə ˈmaʊntɪn]	einen Berg besteigen
to buy a souvenir [ˌbaɪ ə suːvnˈɪə]	ein Souvenir kaufen
to sunbathe on the beach [ˌsʌnbeɪð ɒn ðə ˈbiːtʃ]	sonnenbaden am Strand
to fly to another country [ˌflaɪ tʊ əˌnʌðə ˈkʌntri]	in ein anderes Land fliegen

p. 10	**summer** [ˈsʌmə]	Sommer
	parents *(pl)* [ˈpeərnts]	Eltern
	to **stay** [steɪ]	übernachten; bleiben
	city [ˈsɪti]	Stadt; Großstadt
	to **meet** [miːt], **met** [met]	*hier:* (sich) treffen
	cousin [ˈkʌzn]	Cousin; Cousine
	sang [sæŋ]	simple past von *to sing* (singen)
	to **hear** [hɪə], **heard** [hɜːd]	hören
	to **need** [niːd]	brauchen
	more [mɔː]	mehr
	before [bɪˈfɔː]	bevor
	them [ðem]	sie *(Pl.)*
	to **get married** [ˌget ˈmærɪd]	heiraten
	wedding [ˈwedɪŋ]	Hochzeit
	ate [eɪt]	simple past von *to eat* (essen)
	ice cream [ˌaɪs ˈkriːm]	Eiscreme; Eis
	why [waɪ]	warum
	cricket [ˈkrɪkɪt]	Kricket
	ball [bɔːl]	Ball
	grandfather [ˈgrænˌfɑːðə]	Großvater
	well [wel]	gut
	to **feel** [fiːl], **felt** [felt]	(sich) fühlen
	It's Holly's turn. [ɪts ˈhɒliz ˌtɜːn]	Holly ist dran.
	everyone [ˈevriwʌn]	*hier:* zusammen
	guinea pig [ˈgɪniː pɪg]	Meerschweinchen

p. 12	**aunt** [ɑ:nt]	Tante
	end [end]	Ende; Schluss
	plane [pleɪn]	Flugzeug
p. 13	**grandmother** ['græn,mʌðə]	Großmutter
	gave [geɪv]	simple past von *to give* (geben)
	concert ['kɒnsət]	Konzert
	took [tʊk]	simple past von *to take* (nehmen)
	volleyball ['vɒlibɔ:l]	Volleyball

Station 2

Feelings

surprised [sə'praɪzd]	überrascht
worried ['wʌrid]	beunruhigt; besorgt
angry ['æŋgri]	wütend; zornig; verärgert; böse
excited [ɪk'saɪtɪd]	aufgeregt; begeistert
unhappy [ʌn'hæpi]	unglücklich
afraid [ə'freɪd]	ängstlich
relaxed [rɪ'lækst]	entspannt; locker; gelassen
glad [glæd]	froh
confused [kən'fju:zd]	verwirrt; wirr
nervous ['nɜ:vəs]	nervös; aufgeregt
jealous ['dʒeləs]	eifersüchtig; neidisch

p. 14	**argument** ['ɑ:gjəmənt]	Auseinandersetzung; Streit
	the blue one [ðə 'blu:‿wʌn]	der blaue
	to **borrow** ['bɒrəʊ]	ausleihen
	to **bring** [brɪŋ], **brought** [brɔ:t]	bringen; mitbringen
	to **put** [pʊt], **put** [pʊt]	setzen; legen; stellen

	to **lose** [luːz], **lost** [lɒst]	verlieren
	mine [maɪn]	meins; meine
	when [wen]	wenn; als
	found [faʊnd]	simple past von *to find* (finden)
	to **look** [lʊk]	aussehen; sehen
	like [laɪk]	wie
	hers [hɜːz]	ihre
	That's what happened. [ˌðæts wɒt ˈhæpnd]	Das ist passiert.
	to **happen** [ˈhæpn]	geschehen; passieren
	to **lend** [lend], **lent** [lent]	leihen; verleihen
	so [səʊ]	so
	the same [ðə ˈseɪm]	derselbe; gleich
	as [æz]	wie
	yours [jɔːz]	deine; eure; Ihre
	Never mind. [ˌnevə ˈmaɪnd]	Macht nichts.; Schon gut.; Mach dir nichts draus.
	his [hɪz]	seins; seiner
p. 15	**club** [klʌb]	Klub; Verein
	little [ˈlɪtl]	klein
	What's wrong? [ˌwɒts ˈrɒŋ]	Was ist los?; Was stimmt nicht?
	to **use** [juːz]	benutzen; verwenden
	It doesn't matter. [ɪt ˌdʌznt ˈmætə]	Es ist egal.
	Don't worry. [ˌdəʊnt ˈwʌri]	Mach dir keine Sorgen.
p. 16	**again** [əˈgen]	wieder; noch einmal

Reading corner

p. 18	**lucky day** [ˌlʌki ˈdeɪ]	Glückstag
	sometimes [ˈsʌmtaɪmz]	manchmal
	forgot [fəˈgɒt]	simple past von *to forget* (vergessen)
	on the bus [ˌɒn ðə ˈbʌs]	im Bus
	eye [aɪ]	Auge

	everything ['evriθɪŋ]	alles
	stop [stɒp]	Haltestelle; Halt
	to **get off** [ˌget‿'ɒf], **got off** [ˌgɒt‿'ɒf]	aussteigen
	to **finish** ['fɪnɪʃ]	beenden; enden; aufhören
	company ['kʌmpəni]	Firma; Gesellschaft
	to **ring** [rɪŋ], **rang** [ræŋ]	klingeln; läuten
	to **shout** [ʃaʊt]	schreien; rufen
	door [dɔ:]	Tür
	thing [θɪŋ]	Sache; Ding

Film corner

p. 21	**between** [bɪ'twi:n]	zwischen
	experiment [ɪk'sperɪmənt]	Versuch
	have you got [ˌhæv ju: 'gɒt]	hast du
	comic ['kɒmɪk]	Comic(heft)
	to **ruin** ['ru:ɪn]	ruinieren; zerstören
	break [breɪk], **broke** [brəʊk]	brechen; kaputt machen
	on purpose [ɒn 'pɜ:pəs]	absichtlich
	true [tru:]	wahr
	Stop it! ['stɒp‿ɪt]	Hör(t) auf!
	to **be right** [bi: 'raɪt]	recht haben
	to **be careful** [bi: 'keəfl]	vorsichtig sein
	all right [ˌɔ:l 'raɪt]	in Ordnung; alles klar

Viewing skills

p. 26	**How to …** ['haʊ tə]	Wie man …
	polite [pə'laɪt]	höflich
	scene [si:n]	Szene
p. 27	to **show** [ʃəʊ]	zeigen
	to **get to know** [ˌget tə 'nəʊ]	kennen lernen
	What to … ['wɒt tə]	Was man …
	situation [ˌsɪtju'eɪʃn]	Situation
	best [best]	beste
	queue [kju:]	Warteschlange

escalator ['eskəleɪtə] Rolltreppe
to **wake up** [ˌweɪk‿'ʌp], **woke up** [ˌwəʊk‿'ʌp] aufwachen
to **say sorry** [ˌseɪ 'sɒri] sich entschuldigen

Wenn du ein neues Wort lernst, überlege dir, ob du Wörter zum gleichen Thema kennst, z. B.:

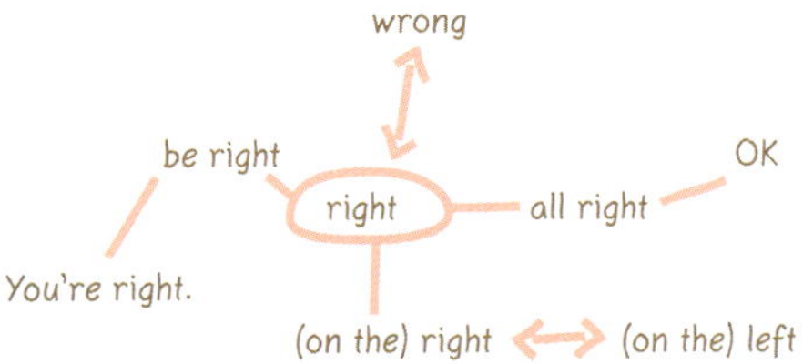

1 Find the words and write them down.

X	S	E	L	A	U	N	T	R
O	Z	S	A	B	W	I	V	S
F	A	N	T	A	S	T	I	C
H	O	L	I	D	A	Y	S	H
D	A	R	Q	C	Y	L	I	A
B	C	F	I	N	E	E	T	T

1. Tante ________________
2. großartig ________________
3. besuchen ________________
4. Hut ________________
5. Ferien ________________
6. schön ________________

2 Make sentences.

1. In the summer my cousins
2. We went to their
3. We stayed in a
4. My dad took lots of
5. My sister went
6. We all visited

a) hotel.
b) London.
c) shopping.
d) wedding.
e) got married.
f) photos.

3 Complete the sentences with family words.

1. Your mum and dad are your ________________________ .
2. Your parents' parents are your ________________________ .
3. Your dad's brother is your ________________________ .
4. Your mum's father is your ________________________ .
5. Your aunt's daughters are your ________________________ .

4 Find the words.

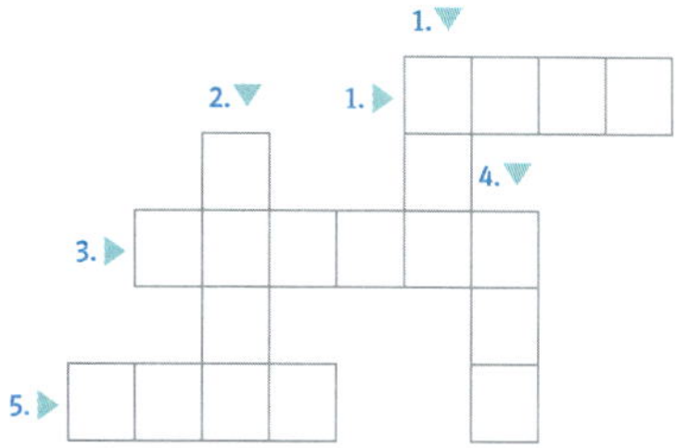

▶ 1. a big town
3. not after
5. You play tennis with this.

▼ 1. You go places in this.
2. "gut" in English
4. The last page is at the … .

5 Find the words and write them.

dissurpre | wordrie | ganry
detexci | pyhaunp | hygrun

1. They aren't so good at cricket. I'm ____________ they won.
2. It's my birthday next week. I'm really ______________ .
3. My brother's got a test tomorrow. He's ________________ about it.
4. My sister lost her mobile and my dad is __________ about it.
5. We're very ________________ because we can't find the cat.
6. Let's have a sandwich. I'm so ______________ .

6 Complete the dialogues.

Olivia: Holly! Is this ________ hat?

Holly: No, it's not ________ . Isn't it Lucy's?

Olivia: No, it isn't ________ . It's very big. Is it ________, Jay?

Jay: No, it isn't ________ hat, but I like it. Can I …?

Olivia: No, you can't, Jay. Is there a name in it?

Holly: Oh yes … here: It says "Luke". Sorry, Jay, it's ________ .

7 Write the words.

1. 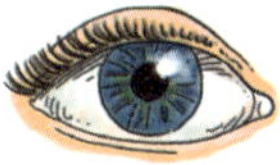

____

2. 

____

3. 

____

4. 

____

5. 

____

6. 

____

8 Write the words in English.

1. alles ________________
2. schreien ________________
3. Firma ________________
4. beenden ________________
5. derselbe ________________
6. noch einmal ________________
7. manchmal ________________

9 Find and write the verbs. Complete the table.

E	N	M	E	T	E	D	R	B	T
A	W	Q	F	E	L	T	Y	R	C
L	B	O	R	R	O	W	G	I	K
U	A	T	E	R	S	T	A	N	D
S	H	A	P	P	E	N	V	G	D
A	F	G	E	T	E	L	E	N	T

German	English infinitive	Simple past
1. ausleihen	________	________
2. bringen	________	________
3. geben	________	________
4. essen	________	________
5. fühlen	________	________
6. geschehen	________	________
7. verleihen	________	________
8. verlieren	________	________
9. treffen	________	________
10. aussteigen	________	________

10 Find the phrases. Complete the dialogues.

1. Why did you do that? – I didn't do it ________________ .
2. He says it's a great comic. – Yes, he ________________ .
3. It's my ____________ . I found some money this morning.
4. I'm sorry I lost your pencil. – It's ________________ .
5. Hey, ____________ . – Oh, I'm sorry.

11 Find the words.

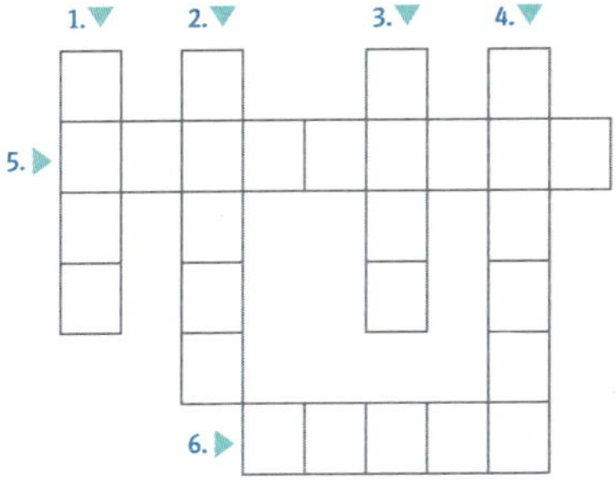

▼ 1. good, better, …
2. The first … of the film is at our school.
3. I usually … up at 7 o'clock.
4. Teacher: Always be … and don't shout.

▶ 5. You can go up on an … .
6. In England people stand in a … at a bus stop.

12 Find the words.

1. My brother is ______________________ of mice.
2. My dad's cool. He's always ______________ about things.
3. We had an argument. I'm __________ we're friends again.
4. We have a test tomorrow. I'm ______________ about it.
5. Ken likes me, but he likes my sister more. I'm __________ .
6. We're ____________________ . What do we have to do?

13 Find the activities and make sentences.

1. 

pack ____________

2. 

buy ____________

3. 

climb ____________

4. 

go ____________

5. 

have ____________

6. 

fly ____________

1. On holiday we meet	a) on the beach.
2. But sometimes we go on	b) in the sea.
3. We love to sunbathe	c) a mountain.
4. It often gets hot so I swim	d) a trip to the sea.
5. Sometimes we fly	e) friends.
6. I love to climb	f) to another country.

Unit 2 Stars!

Way in

p. 28	**star** [stɑː]	Star
	player ['pleɪə]	Spieler; Spielerin
	crowd [kraʊd]	Menschenmenge
	stage [steɪdʒ]	Bühne
	to **organize** ['ɔːgənaɪz]	organisieren
	jumble sale ['dʒʌmbl ˌseɪl]	Flohmarkt
	to **be afraid** [biː ə'freɪd]	sich fürchten; Angst haben
	others ['ʌðəz]	anderen
	You can do it! [juː kæn 'du ɪt]	Du schaffst es!
p. 29	to **draw** [drɔː], **drew** [druː]	zeichnen
	picture ['pɪktʃə]	Bild
	job [dʒɒb]	Aufgabe; Tätigkeit

Station 1

Irregular verbs in Station 1

to **do** [duː]	**did** [dɪd]	**done** [dʌn]	machen; tun
to **see** [siː]	**saw** [sɔː]	**seen** [siːn]	sehen
to **buy** [baɪ]	**bought** [bɔːt]	**bought** [bɔːt]	kaufen
to **feed** [fiːd]	**fed** [fed]	**fed** [fed]	füttern
to **go** [gəʊ]	**went** [went]	**gone** [gɒn]	gehen; fahren
to **hear** [hɪə]	**heard** [hɜːd]	**heard** [hɜːd]	hören
to **take** [teɪk]	**took** [tʊk]	**taken** ['teɪkn]	nehmen; mitnehmen; bringen; mitbringen
to **send** [send]	**sent** [sent]	**sent** [sent]	schicken; senden

to **have** [hæv]	**had** [hæd]	**had** [hæd]	haben
to sweep [swi:p]	swept [swept]	swept [swept]	fegen

Jobs around the house

to **do the shopping** [ˌdu: ðə 'ʃɒpɪŋ]	Einkäufe machen; Besorgungen machen
to **take the rubbish out** [ˌteɪk ðə 'rʌbɪʃ‿aʊt]	den Müll rausbringen
to **tidy (up) your bedroom** [ˌtaɪdi ʌp jɔ: 'bedrʊm]	dein Schlafzimmer aufräumen
to **clean your football boots** [ˌkli:n jɔ: 'fʊtbɔ:l bu:ts]	deine Fußballschuhe putzen
to sweep the floor [ˌswi:p ðə 'flɔ:]	den Fußboden fegen
to lay the table [ˌleɪ ðə 'teɪbl]	den Tisch decken
to do the washing up [ˌdu: ðə 'wɒʃɪŋ‿ʌp]	abspülen
to take bottles to the bottle bank ['teɪk ˌbɒtlz tə ðə 'bɒtl bæŋk]	die Flaschen zum Altglascontainer bringen
to clear the table [ˌklɪə ðə 'teɪbl]	den Tisch abräumen
to hoover my bedroom [ˌhu:və maɪ 'bedrʊm]	mein Schlafzimmer staubsaugen

p. 30	**actor** ['æktə]	Schauspieler; Schauspielerin
	job [dʒɒb]	Job; Arbeit; Beruf
	of course [əv 'kɔ:s]	natürlich; selbstverständlich
	just [dʒʌst]	gerade (eben); soeben
	to **arrive** [ə'raɪv]	ankommen
	already [ɔ:l'redi]	schon; bereits

	to **finish** ['fɪnɪʃ]	fertigstellen; vervollständigen
	list [lɪst]	Liste
	to **wait** [weɪt]	warten
	not … yet [nɒt … 'jet]	noch nicht
	supermarket ['suːpəˌmɑːkɪt]	Supermarkt
	tomorrow (2moro) [tə'mɒrəʊ]	morgen
	to **learn** [lɜːn]	lernen
	lines [laɪnz]	*hier:* Text
	gr8 (great) [greɪt]	großartig; toll
	CU (See you!) ['siː ˌju]	Bis später!
	website ['websaɪt]	Website
p. 31	**bus stop** ['bʌs ˌstɒp]	Bushaltestelle
	You're a star. [ˌjɔːr‿ə 'stɑː]	Du bist fantastisch.
	boot [buːt]	Stiefel
p. 32	**internet** ['ɪntənet]	Internet
p. 33	**DVD** [ˌdiːviː'diː]	DVD
	restaurant ['restrɒnt]	Restaurant
	to **check** [tʃek]	überprüfen; kontrollieren

Station 2

Irregular verbs in Station 2

to **forget** [fə'get]	**forgot** [fə'gɒt]	**forgotten** [fə'gɒtn]	vergessen
to **win** [wɪn]	**won** [wʌn]	**won** [wʌn]	gewinnen; siegen
to **be** [biː]	**was** [wɒz] / **were** [wɜː]	**been** [biːn]	sein
to **make** [meɪk]	**made** [meɪd]	**made** [meɪd]	machen; tun; bilden
to **take** [teɪk]	**took** [tʊk]	**taken** ['teɪkn]	hinbringen
to **eat** [iːt]	**ate** [et/eɪt]	**eaten** ['iːtn]	essen

Jobs

director [dɪ'rektə]	Regisseur; Regisseurin
hairdresser ['heəˌdresə]	Friseur; Friseurin
engineer [ˌendʒɪ'nɪə]	Ingenieur; Ingenieurin; Techniker; Technikerin
waiter ['weɪtə]	Kellner
doctor ['dɒktə]	Arzt; Ärztin
nurse [nɜːs]	Krankenschwester; Krankenpfleger
lorry driver ['lɒri ˌdraɪvə]	LKW-Fahrer; LKW-Fahrerin
builder ['bɪldə]	Bauarbeiter; Bauarbeiterin
shop assistant ['ʃɒp‿əˌsɪstnt]	Verkäufer; Verkäuferin
chef [ʃef]	Koch; Köchin
vet [vet]	Tierarzt; Tierärztin

p. 34	**interview** ['ɪntəvjuː]	Interview; Befragung
	how many [ˌhaʊ 'meni]	wie viele
	to **act** [ækt]	spielen
	ever ['evə]	jemals
	nervous ['nɜːvəs]	nervös; aufgeregt
	embarrassed [ɪm'bærəst]	verlegen
	prize [praɪz]	Preis
	young [jʌŋ]	jung
	Have you ever been to ...? [hæv ju ˌevə 'biːn tə]	Warst du schon in ...?
	Have you finished yet? [ˌhæv juː 'fɪnɪʃt jet]	Seid ihr schon fertig?
	yet [jet]	schon
p. 36	**which** [wɪtʃ]	welche
	grandma ['grænmaː]	Oma
p. 37	**Italy** ['ɪtəli]	Italien
	Spain [speɪn]	Spanien
	Turkey ['tɜːki]	Türkei

	would [wʊd]	würde(n)
	what [wɒt]	welche
	another [ə'nʌðə]	ein andere; noch ein
	would like [wʊd 'laɪk]	würde(n) gern; hätte(n) gern

Reading corner

p. 38	**pantomime** ['pæntəmaɪm]	Weihnachtstheaterstück
	audition [ɔ:'dɪʃn]	Vorspielen; Vorsprechen; Vorsingen; Vortanzen
	a.m. [ˌeɪ'em]	vormittags *(Uhrzeit)*
	p.m. [ˌpi:'em]	nachmittags *(Uhrzeit)*
	theatre ['θɪətə]	Theater
	registration [ˌredʒɪ'streɪʃn]	Anmeldung
	good luck [ˌgʊd 'lʌk]	viel Glück
	behind [bɪ'haɪnd]	hinter
	sofa ['səʊfə]	Sofa
	to **come out** [kʌm‿'aʊt]	hervorkommen
p. 39	**too** [tu:]	zu
	It was my fault. [ɪt wəz ˌmaɪ 'fɔ:lt]	Es war meine Schuld.

Film corner

p. 41	**ticket** ['tɪkɪt]	*hier:* Karte
	acting workshop ['æktɪŋ ˌwɜ:kʃɒp]	Schauspielworkshop
	to **remember** [rɪ'membə]	sich merken; sich erinnern (an)
	just [dʒʌst]	nur
	to **believe** [bɪ'li:v]	glauben
	yourself [jɔ:'self]	dich selbst
	to **panic** ['pænɪk]	panisch werden
	who [hu:]	*hier:* die; welche
	in the world [ɪn ðə 'wɜ:ld]	auf der Welt

Speaking skills

p. 46	**ill** [ɪl]	krank; schlecht
	sore throat [ˌsɔː ˈθrəʊt]	Halsschmerzen
	headache [ˈhedeɪk]	Kopfschmerzen; Kopfweh
	to **have a look** [ˌhæv‿ə ˈlʊk]	anschauen
	to **hurt** [hɜːt], **hurt** [hɜːt], **hurt** [hɜːt]	weh tun; verletzen
	a little [ə ˈlɪtl]	ein bisschen
	to **drink** [drɪŋk], **drank** [dræŋk], **drunk** [drʌŋk]	trinken
	leg [leg]	Bein
	stomach ache [ˈstʌmək ˌeɪk]	Bauchweh; Bauchschmerzen
	broken [ˈbrəʊkn]	past participle von *to break* (brechen; zerbrechen)
p. 47	**mouth** [maʊθ]	Mund
	stomach [ˈstʌmək]	Magen; Bauch
	head [hed]	Kopf
	ear [ɪə]	Ohr
	patient [ˈpeɪʃnt]	Patient; Patientin
	tablet [ˈtæblət]	Tablette
	a lot [əˈlɒt]	sehr

Du kannst die unregelmäßigen Verben mit einem Spiel zu zweit (oder zu mehreren) leichter lernen: Schreibe alle Verbformen jeweils auf einen Zettel und stecke sie in eine Schachtel. Ziehe einen Zettel und sage die Grundform. Sage dann die beiden anderen Verbformen dazu. Dein Partner oder deine Partnerin sagt, wie das Verb auf Deutsch heißt.

A: Drink – drank, drunk.

B: Trinken.

1 Complete the text.

crowd | job | jumble | organized | star | player | stage

My football club wants to go on a trip to Germany.

We needed money so we __________ a __________ sale.

Lots of people came because a famous football __________

was there. He walked to the __________ and spoke to the

__________. He said football was a great sport and he loved

his __________. Everyone was happy and I have a selfie with

the __________. It was great! We can now go to Germany next

summer.

2 Complete the table.

Infinitive	Simple past	Pres. perfect (has / have ...)	German (Infinitive)
1. ______	______	______	kaufen
2. do	______	______	______
3. ______	went	______	______
4. ______	______	heard	______
5. ______	______	______	sehen
6. take	______	______	______

3 Look at the pictures. What has he done?

bought **taken** **cleaned** **done** **tidied**

1. 

He has ______________________________

______________________________ .

2. 

She has ______________________________

______________________________ .

3. 

He has ______________________________

______________________________ .

4. 

She has ______________________________

______________________________ .

5. 

He has ______________________________

______________________________ .

4 Write the right word.

just **already** **(not) yet**

1. Let's go to see the Hobbit. – No, I've ______________ seen it.
2. Have you done your homework? – Yes, I've ______________ finished it now.
3. Have you tidied your room? – No, I haven't done it ________ .

5 Write the text message in words.

____

____

____

____

____

____

____

6 Find the words. Write them next to the German.

A	L	C	B	O	O	T	L	R	C	L
N	I	N	R	U	B	B	I	S	H	E
X	N	F	O	Q	N	N	S	E	B	A
W	E	B	S	I	T	E	T	Z	U	R
J	S	E	D	A	C	T	O	R	L	N
S	U	P	E	R	M	A	R	K	E	T

1. Stiefel – ______________
2. Müll – ______________
3. Text – ______________
4. Liste – ______________
5. Supermarkt – ______________
6. Webseite – ______________
7. Schauspieler – ______________
8. lernen – ______________

7 Write their jobs.

1.  ______________________________

2.  ______________________________

3.  ______________________________

4.  ______________________________

5.  ______________________________

6. 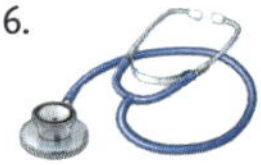 ______________________________

7.  ______________________________

8 Put in the right form of the verb.

1. Where's your homework? – Oh, I'm sorry. I've ______________________ (forget) it.
2. You're late. Where have you ________________ (be)?
3. Yes. It's 2 – 1. United have __________ (win) again!
4. Jill! Where are you? I have just __________ (make) the dinner.

9 Find the words.

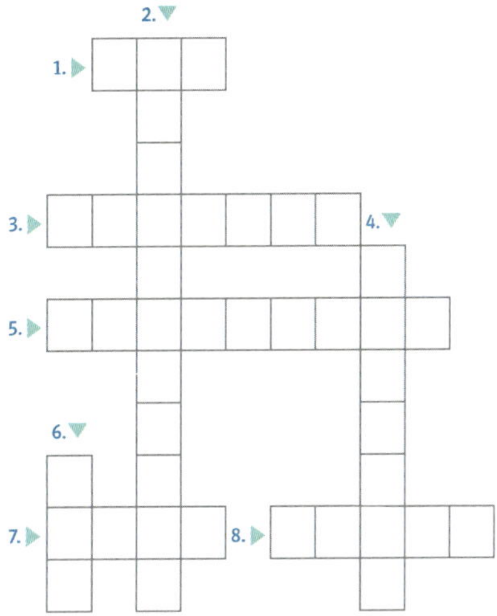

▶ 1. Your dog can't walk? Take him to the … .
3. Your mum's mum is your … .
5. I'm sorry. I've … my homework. I don't usually forget it.
7. Have you … been to Turkey?
8. My grandfather isn't … . He's old.

▼ 2. I fell on stage and I was … .
4. I felt … before I sang my song on stage.
6. Have you done question 8 …?

10 Write the times with a.m. and p.m.

1. 14:00 ____________________
2. 8:00 ____________________
3. 11:59 ____________________
4. 22:15 ____________________

11 What can you see?

1. 

____

2. 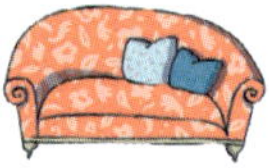

____

3. 

____

4. 

____

12 Write the words in English.

1. sich erinnern — I ____________ you!
2. panisch werden — Don't ____________ ! You're OK.
3. glauben — Do you ____________ in aliens?
4. hervorkommen — ____________ from behind that door!
5. spielen — I want to ____________ in our theatre.

13 Write the words.

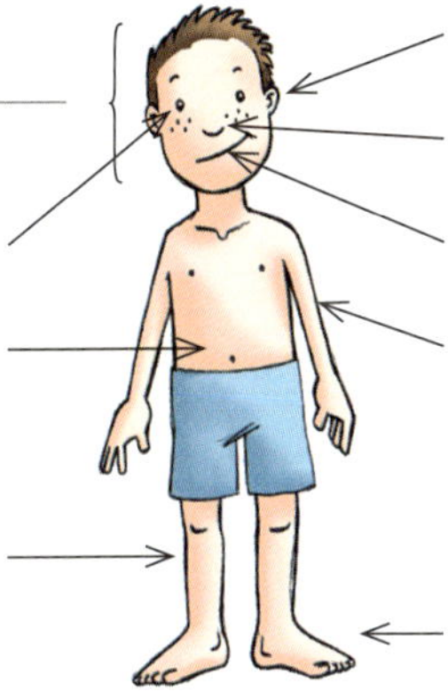

1. ____________
2. ____________
3. ____________
4. ____________
5. ____________
6. ____________
7. ____________
8. ____________
9. ____________

14 Complete the dialogue.

Doctor: Hello Jay. How are you today?

Jay: Oh, I have a stomach __________ and a _________ throat.

Doctor: Does your throat _____________ when you drink?

Jay: Yes, and I have a ______________ .

Doctor: Does your head hurt when you move it?

Jay: Yes, and it hurts when I think. Can you give me some ______________ ?

Doctor: No, Jay. Go home and go to bed and no TV.

Jay: But doctor, I'm not so _________ !

●15 Ready for the party?

a) Find the words.

shwaign pu | ti | oorfl | ecak | telba
lettob nabk | gopnpish | blestot | bushbir

b) Put in the right verb forms and write in the words from a).

Luke has ________ (do) the ________________ and he has ___________ (take) the __________ out! Irina and Jamie have _______ (make) a _______ . Dad has _________ (sweep) the ______ . Mum has already _______ (do) the __________ and has _________ (take) the _________ to the ____________ . Jamie has _______ (lay) the __________ and wants to put the cake on it. But … Oh no! Sherlock has __________ (eat) _____ .

●16 What are their jobs?

1. Anna works in a hospital. She isn't a doctor. ____________________
2. Andy drives a lorry. ____________________
3. Tanya builds houses and flats. ____________________
4. Tom helps people in a shop. ____________________
5. Linda works in a kitchen. ____________________
6. Is your cat ill? Murad can help. ____________________

Unit 3 London Life

Way in

p. 48	**archive** ['ɑ:kaɪv]	Archiv
	blog [blɒg]	Blog; Internettagebuch
	everyone ['evriwʌn]	alle
	back home [bæk 'həʊm]	zu Hause
	Poland ['pəʊlənd]	Polen
	boat trip ['bəʊt ˌtrɪp]	Bootsfahrt; Schiffsfahrt
	sight [saɪt]	Sehenswürdigkeit
	building ['bɪldɪŋ]	Gebäude
	big wheel [ˌbɪg 'wi:l]	Riesenrad
	worker ['wɜ:kə]	Arbeiter; Arbeiterin
	to **build** [bɪld], **built** [bɪlt], **built** [bɪlt]	bauen
p. 49	**the most famous** [ðə 'məʊst ˌfeɪməs]	der berühmteste
	clock tower ['klɒk ˌtaʊə]	Uhrenturm
	clock [klɒk]	Uhr
	tower ['taʊə]	Turm
	step [step]	Stufe
	about [ə'baʊt]	ungefähr; circa; etwa
	prison ['prɪzn]	Gefängnis
	royal ['rɔɪəl]	königlich
	copy ['kɒpi]	Kopie
	It was built … [ˌɪt wəz 'bɪlt]	Es wurde … gebaut.
	writer ['raɪtə]	Schriftsteller; Schriftstellerin
	than [ðæn]	als
	ago [ə'gəʊ]	vor
	really ['rɪəli]	echt
	sure [ʃʊə]	sicher

Station 1

Sights

church [tʃɜ:tʃ]	Kirche
museum [mju:ˈzi:əm]	Museum
castle [ˈkɑ:sl]	Schloss; Burg
stadium [ˈsteɪdiəm]	Stadion
market [ˈmɑ:kɪt]	Markt
town hall [ˌtaʊn ˈhɔ:l]	Rathaus
bridge [brɪdʒ]	Brücke
square [skweə]	Platz
mosque [mɒsk]	Moschee
city centre [ˌsɪti ˈsentə]	Stadtzentrum; Stadtmitte
lake [leɪk]	See
monument [ˈmɒnjəmənt]	Denkmal
lookout point [ˈlʊkaʊt ˌpɔɪnt]	Aussichtspunkt

Numbers 101 – 200,000

a/one hundred and one 101 [ə/wʌn ˌhʌndrəd‿ən ˈwʌn]	hunderteins
a/one hundred and two 102 [ə/wʌn ˌhʌndrəd‿ən ˈtu:]	hundertzwei
a/one hundred and ten 110 [ə/wʌn ˌhʌndrəd‿ən ˈten]	hundertzehn
two hundred 200 [tu: ˈhʌndrəd]	zweihundert
three hundred 300 [θri: ˈhʌndrəd]	dreihundert

	four hundred and fifty-one 451 [fɔː ˈhʌndrəd‿ən ˌfɪftiwʌn]	vierhunderteinundfünfzig
	a / one thousand 1,000 [ə/wʌn ˈθaʊznd]	eintausend

p. 50	**up** [ʌp]	hinauf; oben
	height [haɪt]	Höhe
	fact [fækt]	Fakt; Tatsache
	to **weigh** [weɪ]	wiegen
	tonne [tʌn]	Tonne
	taxi [ˈtæksi]	Taxi
	bell [bel]	Glocke
	dome [dəʊm]	Kuppel
	thought [θɔːt]	simple past, past participle von *to think* (denken)
	tall [tɔːl]	groß; hoch
	as … as [əz … əz]	so … wie
	telephone box [ˈtelɪfəʊn ˌbɒks]	Telefonzelle
	even [ˈiːvn]	noch; sogar
	pretty [ˈprɪti]	hübsch
	expensive [ɪkˈspensɪv]	teuer
	fire [faɪə]	Feuer
p. 51	**TV studio** [ˌtiːˈviː ˌstjuːdiəʊ]	Fernsehstudio
	office [ˈɒfɪs]	Büro
	floor [flɔː]	Stockwerk
	visitor [ˈvɪzɪtə]	Besucher; Besucherin
	low [ləʊ]	niedrig
	to **guess** [ges]	erraten; raten; überlegen
p. 52	**fast** [fɑːst]	schnell
	colourful [ˈkʌləfl]	bunt
	burger [ˈbɜːgə]	Hamburger

Station 2

Adjectives for clothes

cheap [tʃi:p]	billig
expensive [ɪk'spensɪv]	teuer
large [lɑ:dʒ]	groß
small [smɔ:l]	klein
short [ʃɔ:t]	kurz
long [lɒŋ]	lang
tight [taɪt]	eng; fest
loose [lu:s]	locker; lose
fashionable ['fæʃnəbl]	modisch
unfashionable [ʌn'fæʃnəbl]	unmodisch
patterned ['pætənd]	gemustert
plain [pleɪn]	schlicht; einfach
comfortable ['kʌmftəbl]	bequem; angenehm
uncomfortable [ʌn'kʌmftəbl]	unbequem; unangenehm

p. 54	**department store** [dɪ'pɑ:tmənt ˌstɔ:]	Kaufhaus
	sale [seɪl]	Schlussverkauf; Ausverkauf
	top [tɒp]	Top; Oberteil
	department [dɪ'pɑ:tmənt]	Abteilung
	these [ði:z]	diese
	those [ðəʊz]	jene
	to **suit** [su:t]	stehen; passen
	size [saɪz]	Größe
	next [nekst]	als Nächstes
	dress [dres]	Kleid
	isn't it? ['ɪznt‿ɪt]	nicht wahr?; stimmt's?
	may [meɪ]	vielleicht

	in the end [ɪn ði 'end]	schließlich; zum Schluss
	not … any [ˌnɒt … eni]	kein
	shop assistant ['ʃɒp‿əˌsɪstnt]	Verkäufer; Verkäuferin
	receipt [ri'siːt]	Quittung
p. 56	**cute** [kjuːt]	niedlich; süß
	language ['læŋgwɪdʒ]	Sprache
	Scotland ['skɒtlənd]	Schottland
	Europe ['jʊərəp]	Europa
	British ['brɪtɪʃ]	britisch

Reading corner

p. 58	**drama** ['drɑːmə]	Theater; Drama
	play [pleɪ]	Theaterstück
	boss [bɒs]	Boss; Chef
	to **own** [əʊn]	besitzen
	part [pɑːt]	Rolle
	woman *(sg)* ['wʊmən], **women** *(pl)* ['wɪmɪn]	Frau
	landlord ['lændlɔːd]	Eigentümer
	rent [rent]	Miete
	land [lænd]	Land
	builder ['bɪldə]	Bauarbeiter; Bauarbeiterin
	across [ə'krɒs]	über
	heavy ['hevi]	schwer; stark
p. 59	**by** [baɪ]	von
	as [æz]	als
	cannon ['kænən]	Kanone
	cannon ball ['kænən ˌbɔːl]	Kanonenkugel
	to **hit** [hɪt], **hit** [hɪt], **hit** [hɪt]	treffen; schlagen
	roof [ruːf]	Dach
	help [help]	Hilfe
	to **call** [kɔːl]	rufen; anrufen
	fire engine ['faɪər‿ˌendʒɪn]	Feuerwehrauto
	carpenter ['kɑːpəntə]	Zimmermann; Zimmerin; Tischler; Tischlerin
	tool [tuːl]	Werkzeug

Film corner

p. 61	**sunglasses** *(pl)* ['sʌnˌglɑːsɪz]	Sonnenbrille
	to **wait for** [weɪt 'fɔː]	warten auf
	to **go sightseeing** [gəʊ 'saɪtsiːɪŋ]	eine Besichtigungstour machen
	sticker ['stɪkə]	Aufkleber
	stallholder ['stɔːlˌhəʊldə]	Standinhaber; Standinhaberin
	each [iːtʃ]	pro Stück
	a pair of [ə 'peər‿əv]	ein Paar
	price [praɪs]	Preis
	real [rɪəl]	echt; richtig; wirklich
	bargain ['bɑːgɪn]	Schnäppchen
	to **sound** [saʊnd]	klingen

Listening skills

Airport words

departure [dɪ'pɑːtʃə]	Abflug
gate [geɪt]	Gate; Ausgang
last call [ˌlɑːst 'kɔːl]	letzter Aufruf
boarding ['bɔːdɪŋ]	an Bord gehen
cancelled ['kænslt]	annulliert
delayed [dɪ'leɪd]	verspätet
check-in ['tʃekɪn]	Gepäckaufgabe
toilet ['tɔɪlət]	Toilette

p. 66	**airport** ['eəpɔːt]	Flughafen
p. 67	**announcement** [ə'naʊnsmənt]	Durchsage; Ankündigung
	passenger ['pæsndʒə]	Passagier; Passagierin
	plane [pleɪn]	Flugzeug

to **fly** [flaɪ], **flew** [fluː], **flown** [fləʊn]	fliegen
information desk [ɪnfəˈmeɪʃn ˌdesk]	Information

Sammle Wörter, die Ähnlichkeiten oder Unterschiede haben, z.B. Wörter mit zwei Bedeutungen:

Preis ↗ pri**z**e (Gewinn)
Preis ↘ pri**c**e (Kosten)

oder gleich klingende Wörter:

to s**ee** – sehen	s**ea** – Meer
ri**gh**t – richtig	**w**rite – schreiben
to m**ee**t – treffen	m**ea**t – Fleisch
hour – Stunde	our – unser

1 Complete the text.

ago | big wheel | boat trip | clock tower | city | royal | buildings | restaurant | sights | prison | built

Last weekend we went on a day trip to London. One day isn't much time to see the ______ so we started with a __________ __________ on the Thames. You can see a lot of the most famous __________ from the river and a man told us all about them. It was great.

Then we went on the London Eye. That's the __________ on the Thames. They __________ it from 1998 to 2000. The weather was great so we saw most of the famous __________ and parks in London from there. We also saw Big Ben – that's the famous __________ in London.

Then we visited the Tower of London. It was a __________ home and a long time ______ there was a __________ there. In the evening we went to a __________ and ate Indian food. It was great, and next time we want to stay for longer.

2 Write the words next to the German words.

domeevenexpensivefireprettyvisitor

1. sogar ______________
2. hübsch ______________
3. Feuer ______________
4. teuer ______________
5. Kuppel ______________
6. Besucher ______________

It wasn't cheap!

3 Write the words in English and German.

1.  ______________ ______________
2.  ______________ ______________
3.  ______________ ______________
4.  ______________ ______________
5. 

______________ ______________
6.  ______________ ______________
7.  ______________ ______________

4 Write the numbers.

1. 101 ______________________
2. 582 ______________________
3. 334 ______________________
4. 3021 ______________________
5. 9219 ______________________

5 What do you remember? Write the words.

1

________ : 135 metres

It ________ 2,100 ________ .

2

The tower is 96 metres

________ . The ________

weighs 300 kg.

3

It was ________ in 1720.

The ________ has 530 steps.

1. ______________________
2. ______________________
3. ______________________

6 What is it?

1. It's in a building. People work in it. ________________
2. They make TV programmes here. ________________
3. Another word for a tourist. ________________
4. Do this on the beach to get browner. ________________
5. Another word for beautiful. ________________
6. It's information and it's true. ________________

7 Find the words and complete the dialogue.

Jane: What do you think of this ________ ?

Ellen: That colour really ________ you, but it's too small, ________ ?

Jane: Yes, can you ________ the next ________, please?

Ellen: OK … Sorry, I can't see any in size 10.

Jane: Can you ask a ________________, please?

Ellen: Yes, of course … Here, what about ________ jeans?

Jane: Oh, they're great. Thanks!

8 Find six pairs. Write them in English and German.

T	E	X	P	E	N	S	I	V	E
C	J	L	A	N	T	H	I	G	H
H	S	L	L	O	Y	O	U	N	G
E	C	O	L	O	U	R	F	U	L
A	A	W	V	L	U	T	U	P	O
P	T	E	R	B	I	G	L	E	N
F	A	S	M	A	L	L	I	C	G
O	X	O	L	D	R	Y	V	K	I
W	E	T	E	Z	G	R	E	Y	B

1. dry – wet ______ trocken – nass ______
2. ______ ______
3. ______ ______
4. ______ ______
5. ______ ______
6. ______ ______
7. ______ ______

9 Find the words.

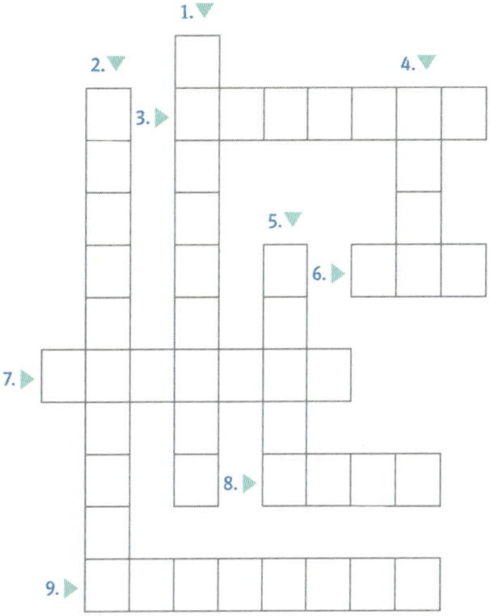

▼
1. This is a woman or man in a car or on a plane.
2. It's sunny so you wear these.
4. Hey! That isn't a … banana. Don't eat it.
5. It's too expensive. The … is too high.

▶
3. Planes leave from an … .
6. I'm going to … to Australia (by plane).
7. Wow, that's cheap. It's a real … .
8. How much are the T-shirts? – Twelve pounds … .
9. I want to put … on my school bag so it looks good.

10 Write the English words.

kael · lofor · rasque · quemso · ontenumm

1. Moschee ________________
2. See ________________
3. Denkmal ________________
4. Platz ________________
5. Stockwerk ________________

11 Write the opposites.

1. tight ________________________________
2. fashionable ________________________________
3. patterned ________________________________
4. comfortable ________________________________

12 Find the wrong word.

1. lake • monument • mosque • theatre
2. floor • roof • square • window
3. act • drama • part • rent
4. loose • monument • plain • tight

13 What can you see in the pictures?

1.  ______________________

2.  ______________________

3.  ______________________

4.  ______________________

5.  ______________________

6.  ______________________

7.  ______________________

14 Write the missing words.

1. My mum's ________ is nice. They work well together.
2. My grandma lives __________ the street from us.
3. My brother has a __________ in the play – he's an alien.
4. My mum works ______ a carpenter.
5. His new play is a __________ , but it's funny too.
6. I want to be an actor __________ I am 16.

Unit 4 Food and drink

Way in

Food

rice [raɪs]	Reis
vegetable (veg) ['vedʒtəbl]	Gemüse
pasta ['pæstə]	Pasta; Nudeln
salad ['sæləd]	Salat
pierogi [pjɜ'rɔgi]	Pirogge
dumpling ['dʌmplɪŋ]	Kloß
cabbage ['kæbɪdʒ]	Kohl; Kraut
sausage ['sɒsɪdʒ]	Wurst; Bratwurst
onion ['ʌnjən]	Zwiebel
pasty ['pæsti]	Pastete
pie [paɪ]	Kuchen; Pastete
potato *(sg)* [pə'teɪtəʊ], **potatoes** *(pl)* [pə'teɪtəʊz]	Kartoffel
carrot ['kærət]	Karotte
chicken ['tʃɪkɪn]	Hühnchen
curry ['kʌri]	Curry
spice [spaɪs]	Gewürz
yogurt ['jɒgət]	Joghurt
bread [bred]	Brot
pork [pɔ:k]	Schweinefleisch
potato salad [pəˌteɪtəʊ 'sæləd]	Kartoffelsalat

p. 68	**drink** [drɪŋk]	Getränk
p. 69	**Jamaican** [dʒə'meɪkən]	jamaikanisch
	sort [sɔ:t]	Sorte; Art

delicious [dɪˈlɪʃəs]	köstlich
it's made with ... [ˌɪts ˈmeɪd wɪð]	es wird aus ... gemacht
dinner [ˈdɪnə]	Mittagessen; Abendessen

Station 1

Irregular verbs in Station 1

to **spend** [spend]	**spent** [spent]	**spent** [spent]	ausgeben; verbringen
to **choose** [tʃuːz]	**chose** [tʃəʊz]	**chosen** [ˈtʃəʊzn]	auswählen; wählen
to **pay** [peɪ]	**paid** [peɪd]	**paid** [peɪd]	bezahlen

Meals at school

packed lunch [ˌpækt ˈlʌnʃ]	Lunchpaket; Vesper
mashed potatoes [ˌmæʃt pəˈteɪtəʊz]	Kartoffelbrei
apple crumble [ˌæpl ˈkrʌmbl]	Apfelauflauf *(mit Streuseln bedeckt)*
custard [ˈkʌstəd]	Vanillesauce
ham [hæm]	Schinken
pasta bake [ˌpæstə ˈbeɪk]	Nudelauflauf
pudding [ˈpʊdɪŋ]	Nachspeise; Pudding
chilli con carne [ˌtʃɪli kɒn ˈkaːni]	Chili con carne
beef [biːf]	Rindfleisch
chilli [ˈtʃɪli]	Chili
garlic [ˈgaːlɪk]	Knoblauch
tomato *(sg)* [təˈmaːtəʊ], **tomatoes** *(pl)* [təˈmaːtəʊz]	Tomate

soup [su:p]	Suppe
strawberry ['strɔ:bri]	Erdbeere
spaghetti [spə'geti]	Spaghetti
sauce [sɔ:s]	Soße
lemon ['lemən]	Zitrone
cheesecake ['tʃi:skeɪk]	Käsekuchen
lasagne [lə'zænjə]	Lasagne
spring roll [ˌsprɪŋ 'rəʊl]	Frühlingsrolle
pancake ['pænkeɪk]	Pfannkuchen
jacket potato [ˌdʒækɪt pə'teɪtəʊ]	Ofenkartoffel
lamb [læm]	Lamm
moussaka [mu'sɑ:kə]	Moussaka

p. 70	**meal** [mi:l]	Mahlzeit; Essen
	news [nju:z]	Neuigkeit(en); Nachricht(en)
	survey ['sɜ:veɪ]	Umfrage
	main course [ˌmeɪn 'kɔ:s]	Hauptgericht
	dessert [dɪ'zɜ:t]	Nachspeise
	usually ['ju:ʒli]	normalerweise; gewöhnlich
	allergy ['ælədʒi]	Allergie
	allergic to [ə'lɜ:dʒɪk tə]	allergisch gegen
	fingerprint ['fɪŋgəprɪnt]	Fingerabdruck
	payment machine ['peɪmənt ˌməʃi:n]	Bezahlautomat
	machine [mə'ʃi:n]	Automat; Maschine
	result [rɪ'zʌlt]	Ergebnis
	many ['meni]	viele
p. 73	**dog biscuit** ['dɒg ˌbɪskɪt]	Hundekeks
	person ['pɜ:sn]	Person; Mensch

Station 2

Things for meals

knife *(sg)* [naɪf], **knives** *(pl)* [naɪvz]	Messer
fork [fɔ:k]	Gabel
spoon [spu:n]	Löffel
salt [sɔ:lt]	Salz
ketchup ['ketʃʌp]	Ketchup
plate [pleɪt]	Teller
glass [glɑ:s]	Glas
pepper ['pepə]	Pfeffer
cup [kʌp]	Tasse
napkin ['næpkɪn]	Serviette
bowl [bəʊl]	Schale; Schälchen; Schüssel
mayonnaise [ˌmeɪə'neɪz]	Mayonnaise
teaspoon ['ti:spu:n]	Teelöffel
straw [strɔ:]	Trinkhalm
mustard ['mʌstəd]	Senf
tray [treɪ]	Tablett
toothpick ['tu:θpɪk]	Zahnstocher

p. 74	**food stall** ['fu:d ˌstɔ:l]	Essensstand
	menu ['menju:]	Speisekarte
	jerk [dʒɜ:k]	*in Gewürzen mariniertes und über Holzfeuer gegrilltes Essen*
	wrap [ræp]	Wrap *(Tortillafladen zum Einwickeln)*
	free range [ˌfri: 'reɪndʒ]	Freiland-
	veggie bean cake [ˌvedʒi 'bi:n keɪk]	vegetarisches Bohnengericht

	mama ['mæmə]	Mama
	fresh [freʃ]	frisch
	combination [ˌkɒmbɪ'neɪʃn]	Kombination
	fried [fraɪd]	(in der Pfanne) gebraten
	plantain ['plæntеɪn]	Kochbanane
	will [wɪl]	werden
	thirsty ['θɜ:sti]	durstig
	juice [dʒu:s]	Saft
	to **order** ['ɔ:də]	bestellen
	anything to drink ['eniθɪŋ tə 'drɪŋk]	etwas zu trinken
	anything ['eniθɪŋ]	irgendetwas
	I've (I have) got [ˌaɪv 'gɒt]	ich habe
	note [nəʊt]	*hier:* Geldschein
	to **pay back** [ˌpeɪ 'bæk]	zurückzahlen
	won't (= will not) [wəʊnt]	nicht werden
	change [tʃeɪndʒ]	Münzgeld; Wechselgeld
	It won't be long. [ɪt ˌwəʊnt bi 'lɒŋ]	Es wird nicht lange dauern.
	over there [ˌəʊvə 'ðeə]	da drüben; dort drüben
p. 75	**tuna** ['tju:nə]	Thunfisch
	extra ['ekstrə]	zusätzlich; Zusatz-
p. 76	**any** ['eni]	irgendwelche; irgendein
	shirt [ʃɜ:t]	Hemd; Shirt
p. 77	to **watch** [wɒtʃ]	*hier:* aufpassen auf

Reading corner

p. 78	to **cook** [kʊk]	kochen
	TV show [ˌti:'vi: ˌʃəʊ]	Fernsehsendung
	teen [ti:n]	Jugend-; Teenager; Jugendliche; Jugendlicher
	chef [ʃef]	Koch; Köchin
	kid [kɪd]	Kind
	judge [dʒʌdʒ]	Juror; Jurorin
	entry form ['entri ˌfɔ:m]	Anmeldeformular
	scrambled egg [ˌskræmbld‿'eg]	Rührei

	to **watch** [wɒtʃ]	zuschauen
	magic ['mædʒɪk]	Magie; Zauberei
	to **become** [bɪ'kʌm], **became** [bɪ'keɪm], **become** [bɪ'kʌm]	werden
	catering college ['keɪtərɪŋ ˌkɒlɪdʒ]	Hotelfachschule
	teamwork ['ti:mwɜ:k]	Teamwork
	I prefer working [aɪ prɪ'fɜ: ˌwɜ:kɪŋ]	ich arbeite lieber
	advice [əd'vaɪs]	Rat; Ratschlag
	hard [hɑ:d]	hart
	head chef ['hed ˌʃef]	Chefkoch
p. 79	**recipe** ['resɪpi]	Rezept
	of mine [əv 'maɪn]	von mir
	ingredient [ɪn'gri:diənt]	Zutat
	milk [mɪlk]	Milch
	piece [pi:s]	Stück
	pinch [pɪntʃ]	*hier:* Prise
	to **add** [æd]	hinzufügen
	to **stir** [stɜ:]	rühren; umrühren
	microwave ['maɪkrəweɪv]	Mikrowelle
	second ['seknd]	Sekunde
	tablespoon ['teɪblspu:n]	Esslöffel
	once more ['wʌns ˌmɔ:]	noch einmal

Film corner

p. 81	to **twist** [twɪst]	verdrehen; verzerren
	ankle ['æŋkl]	Fußgelenk; Fußknöchel
	basketball ['bɑ:skɪtbɔ:l]	Basketball
	to **pass** [pɑ:s]	reichen
	lemonade [ˌlemə'neɪd]	Limonade
	Help yourselves! [ˌhelp jɔ:'selvz]	Bedient euch!; Bedienen Sie sich!
	lovely ['lʌvli]	schön; herrlich; hübsch
	may [meɪ]	dürfen; können
	sausage roll [ˌsɒsɪdʒ 'rəʊl]	*Blätterteig mit Wurstfüllung*

Reading skills

p. 86	**Indian** [ˈɪndiən]	indisch
	message [ˈmesɪdʒ]	Nachricht; SMS
	flyer [ˈflaɪə]	Flyer; Faltblatt
	dish [dɪʃ]	Gericht; Speise
	takeaway [ˈteɪkəweɪ]	Essen zum Mitnehmen
p. 87	**to** [tʊ]	*hier:* bis

Fertige für jede Präposition (after, about, to etc.) eine Karteikarte an und schreibe passende Wortverbindungen dazu:

on
- on purpose
- on the right / left
- on Friday

after
- to look after
- after that

to
- allergic to
- quarter to five

1 Write the food words.

2 Write the missing words.

My ____________ makes my favourite food. She's ________

and she always uses special __________ . She makes a ____

of curry which is __________ . It has fish, vegetables and

__________ in it.

3 Complete the table.

Infinitive	Simple past	Pres. perfect (has / have ...)	German (Infinitive)
1. ________	________	________	auswählen
2. spend	________	________	________
3. ________	flew	________	________
4. ________	________	paid	________

4 Find the words and write them in the right order.

anim oscure 1. ____________________

redsset 2. ____________________

dingdup 3. ____________________

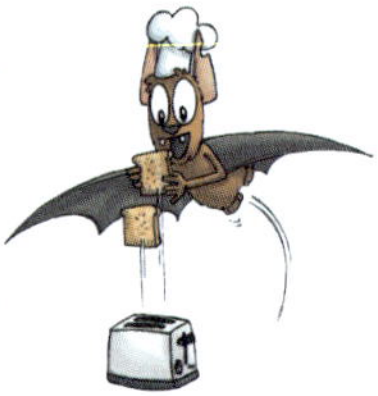

5 Match the words.

1. packed crumble
2. mashed lunch
3. apple bake
4. pasta potatoes

6 Write the words.

Dave Preston often eats a school dinner in the cafeteria and he u__________ spends £3.00. He loves sausages and m______________ p______________ for his main course. He can't eat nuts because he is a_____________ to them. Yesterday he s________ £4.00 at the p___________ machine because he ate two delicious d__________ .

7 Complete the sentences with the English words.

1. Nachrichten Did you hear the _________ yesterday?
2. viele We don't have _________ tomatoes.
3. Essen What's your favourite ___________ ?
4. gebraten I love ___________ bananas.

8 Find the words.

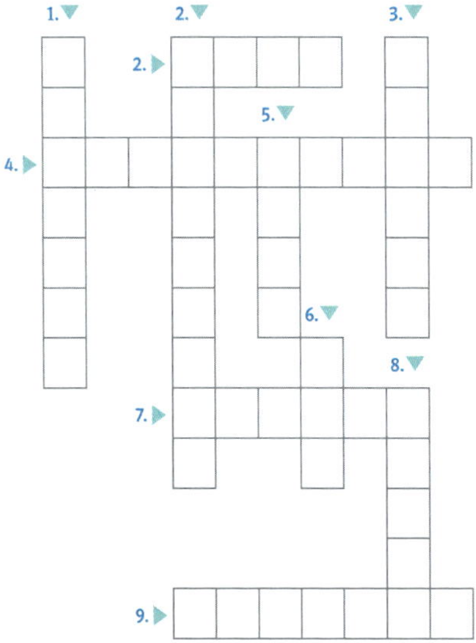

▶ 2. Eat this before the main course.
4. a small red fruit
7. It's red and you eat it in salads.
9. another word for dessert

▼ 1. Eat this warm or cold on desserts.
2. They eat this a lot in Italy.
3. a vegetable; like an onion
5. meat from a cow
6. another meat
8. like garlic; hurts your eyes

9 What are the words?

1. ______________________
2. ______________________
3. ______________________
4. ______________________
5. ______________________
6. ______________________

10 Find the wrong word and write it in German.

1. pennies • change • extra • note — *zusätzlich / Zusatz-*
2. plantain • ketchup • pepper • salt ______________________
3. apple • banana • plantain • wrap ______________________
4. free range • fresh • napkin • spicy ______________________
5. combination • fork • knife • spoon ______________________
6. cup • menu • glass • plate ______________________
7. juice • tea • thirsty • water ______________________
8. beef • ham • order • pork ______________________

11 Find the words. Write them next to the German.

V	C	I	T	E	E	N	L	A	S
J	T	R	E	C	I	P	E	N	I
U	C	I	D	H	M	I	L	K	K
D	R	T	S	E	C	E	N	U	I
G	Y	O	N	F	E	C	B	D	D
E	W	A	T	C	H	E	K	A	N

1. Jugendliche – ____________
2. zuschauen – ____________
3. Rezept – ____________
4. Koch – ____________
5. Juror – ____________
6. Kind – ____________
7. Stück – ____________
8. Milch – ____________

12 Write the verbs.

1. kochen — Do you often ____________ at home?
2. werden — I want to ____________ a chef.
3. vorziehen — Do you ____________ meat or fish?
4. hinzufügen — I think we need to ____________ some salt!

Do you want to become a chef?

13 Match the sentence parts.

1. My mum twisted	a) of cake.
2. We often eat scrambled	b) yourselves!
3. Can you pass	c) the salt, please?
4. I'd like a piece	d) eggs.
5. Help	e) her ankle last week.

14 Find eight words for nice.

1. g __ __ d	5. g r __ __ t
2. d __ l __ c __ __ __ s	6. l __ v __ l y
3. p r __ t t y	7. b __ __ __ t __ f __ l
4. b r __ l l __ __ n t	8. f __ n t __ s t __ c

15 Find the words and complete the sentences.

We love __________ food. We often get a ______________ from the restaurant. We have a __________ with their menu so we can ____________ by phone. We also have a _______________ book with our favourite __________ .

Then we eat it at home.

16 Write the words and find the salad sauce.

1. A dessert with apples? _ _ _ _ ☐ _ _ _ _ _ _ _ _
2. Eat your dinner on this? _ _ _ ☐
3. It's a yellow fruit. _ _ ☐ _ _
4. Eat this as a main course with cheese and ham or with sugar as a dessert. _ _ ☐ _ _ _ _
5. A yellow sauce. Eat it with sausages. _ _ _ _ ☐ _ _
6. It's a young sheep. _ ☐ _ _
7. It has vegetables and / or meat inside. It's not a wrap or a pie! _ _ _ ☐ _ _ / _ _ _ _
8. An Italian dish! It's made of pasta, meat and cheese sauce. _ _ _ _ _ ☐ _
9. It's made with cheese and sugar. Eat it for dessert. _ _ _ _ ☐ _ _ _ _ _
10. A spoon for a drink? _ _ _ _ _ ☐ _ _

A white sauce for salads? _ _ _ _ _ _ _ _ _ _

17 Find more food words.

1. wastr ______________________
2. lowb ______________________
3. massakou ______________________
4. thickpoot ______________________

18 Find the right words.

romf | niem | fech | grokwin | gleecol

1. He's the head ______________ .
2. She's at catering ____________ .
3. He's a friend of _____________ .
4. Can I have an entry __________ , please?
5. I prefer ________________ in my kitchen.

19 Match the parts.

1. stir
2. add
3. give me

a) some advice
b) the soup
c) a pinch of salt

20 Find the words and write them in German.

1. ______________________________
2. ______________________________
3. ______________________________
4. ______________________________
5. ______________________________

Unit 5 In the news

Way in

p. 88	**TTYL (Talk to you later!)** ['tɔ:k tə ju ˌleɪtə]	Wir reden später!
	Good morning. [ˌgʊd 'mɔ:nɪŋ]	Guten Morgen.
	gamer ['geɪmə]	Spieler *(Computer)*; Spielerin *(Computer)*
	to **stand** [stænd], **stood** [stʊd], **stood** [stʊd]	stehen
	fantasy ['fæntəsi]	Fantasie; Fantasy
p. 89	to **travel** ['trævl]	reisen
	through [θru:]	durch
	treasure ['treʒə]	Schatz
p. 88	**difficult** ['dɪfɪklt]	schwierig
p. 89	**LOL (Laugh out loud!)** ['lɑ:f aʊt ˌlaʊd]	Laut lachen!
	to **laugh** [lɑ:f]	lachen
	kiss [kɪs]	Kuss

Station 1

Media

to **chat** [tʃæt]	chatten; plaudern
online [ˌɒn'laɪn]	online
to **surf the internet** [ˌsɜ:f ði 'ɪntənet]	im Internet surfen
to **download** [ˌdaʊn'ləʊd]	herunterladen
to **upload** ['ʌpləʊd]	ins Internet stellen; hochladen
to **bookmark** ['bʊkmɑ:k]	zu … hinfügen
to **copy** ['kɒpi]	kopieren

to paste [peɪst]	einfügen
to save [seɪv]	speichern
file [faɪl]	Datei
text [tekst]	Text
video ['vɪdiəʊ]	Video
comment ['kɒment]	Kommentar
software ['sɒftweə]	Software

p. 91 **jacket** ['dʒækɪt] Jacke

Station 2

Activities

to **rap** [ræp]	rappen
to **try on** [ˌtraɪ 'ɒn]	anprobieren
to **hang (around)** [hæŋ], **hung** [hʌŋ], **hung** [hʌŋ]	(herum)hängen
to **ride (a bike)** [raɪd], **rode** [rəʊd], **ridden** ['rɪdn]	(Fahrrad) fahren
to get dressed [ˌget 'drest]	sich anziehen
to repair [rɪ'peə]	reparieren
to talk to a neighbour ['neɪbə]	mit dem Nachbar reden
to have a haircut ['heəkʌt]	sich die Haare schneiden lassen
to paint [peɪnt]	streichen; anmalen; malen
to take a break [ˌteɪk‿ə 'breɪk]	Pause machen

p. 94 **moment** ['məʊmənt] Moment; Augenblick
while [waɪl] während

	clever ['klevə]	schlau; klug; intelligent
	to **wave** [weɪv]	winken
p. 97	**I think so.** [ˌaɪ 'θɪŋk səʊ]	Ich glaube.
	Your turn. [ˌjɔː 'tɜːn]	Du bist dran.

Reading corner

p. 98	**dream** [driːm]	Traum
	to **test** [test]	testen; prüfen
	roller coaster ['rəʊlə ˌkəʊstə]	Achterbahn
	ride [raɪd]	Fahrt; Ritt
	children ['tʃɪldrən]	Kinder
	billion ['bɪliən]	Milliarde
	to **fit** [fɪt]	passen
	island ['aɪlənd]	Insel
	to **be called** [biː 'kɔːld]	heißen; genannt werden
p. 99	**South Pole** ['saʊθ ˌpəʊl]	Südpol
	to **ski** [skiː]	Ski fahren
	mile [maɪl]	Meile
	to **rest** [rest]	rasten; ausruhen; liegen
	hard [hɑːd]	schwer; schwierig
	to **swim** [swɪm], **swam** [swæm], **swum** [swʌm]	schwimmen
	way to go ['weɪ tə ˌgəʊ]	super
	America [ə'merɪkə]	Amerika
	texter ['tekstə]	SMS-Schreiber; SMS-Schreiberin
	wrote [rəʊt]	simple past von *to write* (schreiben)
	text [tekst]	Text
	minute ['mɪnɪt]	Minute
	to **text** [tekst]	texten; eine SMS schreiben

Film corner

p. 101	**What about you?** [ˌwɒt‿əbaʊt ˈjuː]	Und du?
	to **agree** [əˈgriː]	zustimmen
	to **disagree** [ˌdɪsəˈgriː]	anderer Meinung sein; nicht einverstanden sein
	I don't think so. [ˌaɪ dəʊnt ˈθɪŋk səʊ]	Ich glaube nicht.
	part [pɑːt]	Teil

Writing skills

p. 106	**suddenly** [ˈsʌdnli]	plötzlich; auf einmal
	wall [wɔːl]	Mauer; Wand
	out [aʊt]	heraus
	lettuce [ˈletɪs]	Kopfsalat
	finally [ˈfaɪnli]	schließlich; zum Schluss
p. 107	**at last** [ət ˈlɑːst]	endlich; zu guter Letzt
	to **understand** [ˌʌndəˈstænd], **understood** [ˌʌndəˈstʊd], **understood** [ˌʌndəˈstʊd]	verstehen

Verwende verschiedene Farben, um dir schwierige Wörter zu merken, z. B.:
gelb – die Aussprache fällt mir schwer
blau – die Rechtschreibung finde ich nicht so leicht
grün – die Bedeutung kann ich mir schlecht merken
Diese Wörter wiederholst du dann, bis du sie dir gut eingeprägt hast.

1 Write the text message.

____

____

____

____

____

____

2 Write the words.

1. This person plays computer games. ________________
2. You say this when you get up. ________________
3. This is not easy. ________________
4. Something you really want or like. ________________
5. This is not real. ________________
6. You do this when you hear a good joke. ________________
7. Your mum may give you one of these. ________________
8. You can write this on your mobile. ________________

3 Match the words.

1. chat	a) a text message
2. surf	b) to music
3. write	c) online
4. read	d) the internet
5. listen	e) a book

4 Complete the sentences.

a) Match the words.

try	hang	has	on the
wait	ride	for	got
on	my bike	bus	around

b) Complete the sentences with the sentence parts from a).

1. I'd like to __________ this jacket, please. – Yes, of course. Is that your size?
2. I __________________________ in the park and __________________________ on Saturdays.
3. I met your brother __________________ yesterday.
4. My sister __________ that new game.
5. I don't want to walk. Let's ________________ the bus.

5 Find the verbs. Write them next to the German.

1. lachen – ____________________
2. reisen – ____________________
3. stehen – ____________________
4. plaudern – ____________________
5. rappen – ____________________
6. winken – ____________________
7. (an)rufen – ____________________

C	A	L	L	P
S	T	A	N	D
O	R	U	D	A
W	A	G	C	S
A	V	H	H	T
V	E	R	A	P
E	L	W	T	Y

6 Complete the table.

Infinitive	Simple past	Pres. perfect (has / have ...)	German (Infinitive)
1. ________	________	________	hängen
2. ride	________	________	________
3. ________	stood	________	________
4. ________	________	swum	________

7 Write the words.

1. Augenblick ____________
2. während ____________
3. schlau ____________

8 Find the words.

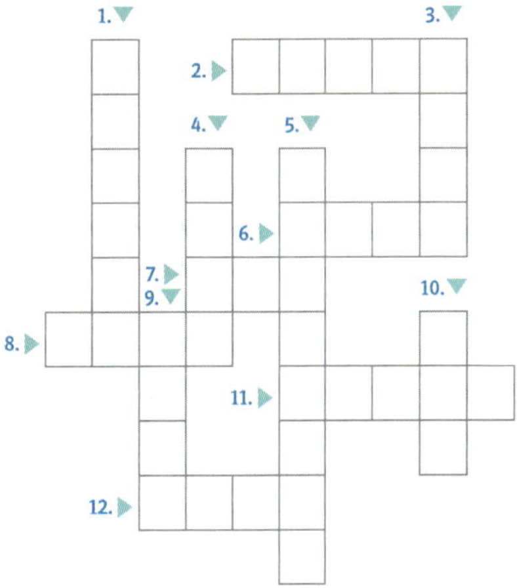

▶
2. You … at a funny joke.
6. … is another word for difficult.
7. People … in the mountains in winter.
8. At one shop you can … new games before you buy them.
11. I had a funny … last night.
12. A … is longer than a kilometre.

▼
1. When you surf the internet, you are … .
3. Your eyes and nose are on your … .
4. After you work for a long time, you need to … .
5. Boys and girls are … .
9. I often … at the swimming pool.
10. They don't really sing. They speak and sing: They … .

9 Find the words and write them in the dialogue.

Bob: Did you buy that new game yesterday?

Helen: Yes, I bought it in the morning. ________________ ?

Bob: Oh, it was awful. We didn't get to the shop until 4 p.m. and there weren't any more games there. We looked and looked and ______________ we found one!

Helen: Did Janet get one too?

Bob: No, ________________ . She doesn't think it's good.

Helen: Oh, ____________________ . I think it's great!

10 Write the words.

1.  ______________________________

2.  ______________________________

3.  ______________________________

4.  ______________________________

5.  ______________________________

6.  ______________________________

● 11 Complete the text with computer words.

I use the internet a lot. I d__________ songs and v__________ so that I can watch them on long trips. I often write a c__________ about the videos I watch. I think that people like to read them. I download s__________ for my computer so I don't need to buy it in a shop.

I also find information for my homework on the internet. I copy it and s__________ it as a f__________ on my computer so that I can read the information again later. I NEVER c__________ and p__________ it into my homework, of course!

● 12 Write the verbs.

1. sich anziehen — I __________________ after breakfast.
2. reparieren — Can you __________________ my bike, please?
3. streichen — I want to __________________ my bedroom green.
4. hochladen — Don't __________________ that photo on Facebook!
5. passen — These books won't __________________ in my bag.
6. zustimmen — Yes, I __________________ . It was a good film.

Unit 6 Goodbye Greenwich

Way in

p. 109	to **leave** [li:v], **left** [left], **left** [left]	abfahren; verlassen; lassen
	soon [su:n]	bald
	to **miss** [mɪs]	vermissen
	away [ə'weɪ]	weg; entfernt
	guys [gaɪz]	Leute
	side [saɪd]	Seite
	chance [tʃɑ:ns]	Chance; Gelegenheit; Möglichkeit
	Cornish ['kɔ:nɪʃ]	Cornish; aus Cornwall
	smuggler ['smʌglə]	Schmuggler; Schmugglerin
	the best [ðə 'best]	die besten
p. 108	**sand** [sænd]	Sand
	harbour ['hɑ:bə]	Hafen
	to **move (house)** [mu:v]	umziehen
p. 109	**Congratulations!** [kənˌgrætʃu'leɪʃnz]	Glückwunsch!
	Well done! [ˌwel 'dʌn]	Gut gemacht!

Station 1

Holiday activities

to **make jewellery** [ˌmeɪk 'dʒu:əlri]	Schmuck machen
to **go camping** [ˌgəʊ 'kæmpɪŋ]	campen gehen; zelten
to **go beach combing** [gəʊ 'bi:tʃ ˌkəʊmɪŋ]	den Strand nach Strandgut absuchen
to sleep in a tent [ˌsli:p ɪn‿ə 'tent]	in einem Zelt schlafen

to surf on a big wave [ˌsɜːf ɒn‿ə bɪɡ ˈweɪv]	auf einer großen Welle surfen
to hike in the woods [ˌhaɪk ɪn ðə ˈwʊdz]	im Wald wandern gehen
to swim in a stream [ˌswɪm ɪn‿ə ˈstriːm]	in einem Bach schwimmen

p. 110	**plan** [plæn]	Plan
	three more days [ˌθriː mɔː ˈdeɪz]	noch drei Tage
	before [bɪˈfɔː]	*hier:* bis zu
	camp [kæmp]	Camp; Lager
	jealous [ˈdʒeləs]	eifersüchtig; neidisch
	before [bɪˈfɔː]	vorher; zuvor
	leaving [ˈliːvɪŋ]	Abschieds-
	to **plan** [plæn]	planen
p. 111	**table tennis** [ˈteɪbl ˌtenɪs]	Tischtennis
	to **look after** [ˌlʊk‿ˈɑːftə]	aufpassen; hüten
	slept [slept]	simple past, past participle von *to sleep* (schlafen)
	to **sell** [sel], **sold** [səʊld], **sold** [səʊld]	verkaufen
p. 113	**umbrella** [ʌmˈbrelə]	Regenschirm

Station 2

Farewell

farewell speech [feəˈwel spiːtʃ]	Abschiedsrede
to change school [ˌtʃeɪndʒ ˈskuːl]	die Schule wechseln
to pack up things [ˌpæk‿ʌp ˈθɪŋz]	Sachen packen
to say goodbye [ˈseɪ ˌɡʊdˈbaɪ]	sich verabschieden

to **explore** [ɪk'splɔ:]	erkunden; erforschen
to **feel at home quickly** [ˌfi:l ət ˌhəʊm 'kwɪkli]	sich schnell zu Hause fühlen
to **have a new address** [ˌhæv‿ə nju: ə'dres]	eine neue Adresse haben
to **keep in touch** [ˌki:p ɪn 'tʌtʃ]	in Verbindung bleiben
to **keep** [ki:p], **kept** [kept], **kept** [kept]	halten

p. 114	**flag** [flæg]	Flagge; Fahne
	scone [skɒn]	Scone *(eine Art süßes Brötchen)*
	Is something wrong? [ɪz 'sʌmθɪŋ rɒŋ]	Stimmt etwas nicht?
	a bit [ə 'bɪt]	ein bisschen; ein wenig
	maybe ['meɪbi]	vielleicht
	or [ɔ:]	oder
	if [ɪf]	wenn
	to **hope** [həʊp]	hoffen
	silly ['sɪli]	albern
	forever [fə'revə]	für immer; ewig
p. 116	to **pack** [pæk]	packen; einpacken
	too much [ˌtu: 'mʌtʃ]	zu sehr

Reading corner

p. 118	**secret** ['si:krət]	Geheimnis
	cave [keɪv]	Höhle
	only ['əʊnli]	einzige
	strange [streɪndʒ]	merkwürdig; seltsam
	this way [ðɪs 'weɪ]	in diese Richtung
	rock [rɒk]	Fels; Stein
	to **watch** [wɒtʃ]	*hier:* beobachten

p. 119 **now** [naʊ] — *hier:* heutzutage
against [ə'genst] — gegen
secret ['si:krət] — geheim

Film corner

p. 121 **inside** [ˌɪn'saɪd] — in … hinein
ghost [gəʊst] — Geist
to **scare** [skeə] — erschrecken

*Spielt zu zweit das **Jobs und activities** Spiel.
Schreibt folgende Wörter jeweils auf einen Zettel, lasst aber die letzten zwei Buchstaben weg – z.B.*

build __ __ | play __ __

build**er**	driv**er**
offic**er**	carpent**er**
play**er**	caretak**er**
hairdress**er**	smuggl**er**
stallhold**er**	teach**er**
wait**er**	writ**er**
gam**er**	act**or**
farm**er**	direct**or**
sing**er**	doct**or**
danc**er**	visit**or**

Steckt alle Zettel in eine Schachtel. Zieht abwechselnd einen Zettel und sagt das ganze Wort und wie man es schreibt: mit -er oder -or.

1 Write the words and find a place in England.

1. Things and people from Cornwall are … . ▢_ _ _ _ _▢
2. Tomorrow is … . Next year is not. _ _ _▢
3. Long ago … lived in Cornwall. They brought things to England by boat. _ _ _ _ _ _ _ _▢_
4. Cornwall is miles … from London. _▢_ _
5. … is another word for people. "Well done, … !" ▢_ _ _
6. What time do you … school? … is another word for "go away". _▢_ _ _
7. My best friend moved to Australia last year and I still … her. _▢_ _
8. I'm a United fan. They are … . _ _ _ _▢_ _

The place in England is _ _ _ _ _ _ _ _ _ .

2 Write the words or phrases in English.

1. Plan	I have a good ____________ !	
2. nach drei Tage	In ____________________ it's my birthday.	
3. Abschieds-	When is your ____________ party?	
4. neidisch	He's got a new mobile. I'm ________ .	
5. zuvor	I want a big party ________ I leave.	
6. Glückwünsch	______________________ ! You won.	

3 Look at the pictures. Complete the sentences.

1.

We often go ______________ .

4.

She's making ______________ .

2.

We love to go ______________ .

5.

We often ______________ .

3.

We need my ______________ .

6.

I ______________ my brother.

4 Match the words and write the sentences.

1. Is something	much!	______________
2. This is my farewell	wrong?	______________
3. Hmm. I love your	bit?	______________
4. Don't eat too	scones!	______________
5. Would you like a	speech.	______________

5 Complete the table.

Infinitive	Simple past	Pres. perfect (has / have ...)	German (Infinitive)
1. ______	______	______	zustimmen
2. leave	______	______	______
3. ______	missed	______	______
4. ______	______	stood	______
5. ______	______	______	verstehen
6. wave	______	______	______

6 Describe the people.

a) Find the words.

levecr | lilsy | souljea
hirtsyt | shefr | darh

b) Match the words from a) with the right person or thing.

1. Al understands things. He's good at school.

   He's ______________ .

2. Rob often does crazy things. He never thinks.

   He's ______________ .

3. Mike's girlfriend likes another boy.

   He's ______________ .

4. Mary went on a long walk. Now she needs a drink.

   She's ______________ .

5. These apples were on the tree a minute ago.

   They're ______________ .

6. This question isn't easy. I can't do it.

   It's ______________ .

7 Write the words in English.

1. alle ______________
2. vielleicht ______________
3. ewig ______________

8 Match the sentence parts.

1. Let's go this — a) I'll be unhappy.
2. When we move, — b) way.
3. Let's watch — c) touch.
4. Let's keep in — d) a film.

9 Write the words.

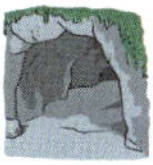

1. ______________

2. ______________

3. ______________

4. ______________

5. ______________

6. ______________

10 Find 12 words. Write them next to the German.

S	T	R	A	N	G	E	O	U	P
E	A	I	G	L	Z	F	T	M	R
C	S	C	A	R	E	Q	O	B	D
R	Y	R	I	B	E	F	O	R	E
E	F	I	N	S	I	D	E	E	W
T	L	A	S	C	O	N	E	L	N
Y	A	K	T	Y	S	I	L	L	Y
S	G	G	H	O	S	T	I	A	M

1. Fahne ______________
2. Geist ______________
3. Quietsch ______________
4. gegen ______________
5. albern ______________
6. bis zu ______________
7. ein süßes Brötchen ______________
8. Geheimnis ______________
9. seltsam ______________
10. Regenschirm ______________
11. in … hinein ______________
12. erschrecken ______________

● 11 Write the missing words.

We often go camping in Cornwall in the summer. We all love to sleep in a ________ even when it rains. We go to the beach if we can. We go beach ________ and we love to surf on big ________ when it's windy. When it rains, we hike in the ________ or walk on rocks in little ________ . Sometimes we ________ old castles.

Holidays are great but I didn't want to move there. Now I have to change ________ and say ________ to my friends. Next we must ________ up our things and we'll have a new ________ . I may ________ at home quickly but I think I'll miss my friends ________ .

● 12 Write the words.

1. Fels ________
2. seltsam ________
3. heutzutage ________
4. Adresse ________
5. einzige ________
6. verkaufen ________

Unit 1

1 1. aunt, 2. fantastic, 3. visit, 4. hat, 5. holiday, 6. fine

2 1. e), 2. d), 3. a), 4. f), 5. c), 6. b)

3 1. parents, 2. grandparents, 3. uncle, 4. grandfather, 5. cousins

4 → 1. city, 3. before, 5. ball ↓ 1. car, 2. well, 4. end

5 1. surprised, 2. excited, 3. worried, 4. angry, 5. unhappy, 6. hungry

6 your, mine, hers, yours, my, his

7 1. eye, 2. door, 3. ball, 4. guinea pig, 5. bus stop, 6. ice cream

8 1. everything, 2. shout, 3. company, 4. finish, 5. the same, 6. again, 7. sometimes

9 1. borrow, borrowed, 2. bring, brought, 3. give, gave, 4. eat, ate, 5. feel, felt, 6. happen, happened, 7. lend, lent, 8. lose, lost, 9. meet, met, 10. get off, got off

10 1. on purpose, 2. is right, 3. lucky day, 4. all right, 5. stop it

11 ↓ 1. best, 2. scene, 3. wake, 4. polite
→ 5. escalator, 6. queue

● 12 1. afraid, 2. relaxed, 3. glad, 4. nervous, 5. jealous, 6. confused

● 13 1. pack (a suitcase), 2. buy souvenirs / a souvenir, 3. climb (a mountain), 4. go on a trip, 5. have a picnic, 6. fly (to another country)
1. e), 2. d), 3. a), 4. b), 5. f), 6. c)

Unit 2

1 1. organised, jumble, player, stage, crowd, job, star

2 1. buy, bought, bought – kaufen, 2. do, did, done – tun, 3. go, went, gone – gehen, 4. hear, heard, heard – hören, 5. see, saw, seen – sehen, 6. take, took, taken – nehmen

3 1. He has done the shopping. 2. She has taken the rubbish out. 3. He has tidied his room. 4. She has cleaned her football boots. 5. He has bought a (foot)ball.

4 1. already, 2. just, 3. yet

5 Hi Luke, Where are you? You are late. The film has started. It's great. See you in the cinema or at my house tomorrow? Dave

6 1. boot, 2. rubbish, 3. lines, 4. list, 5. supermarket, 6. website, 7. actor, 8. learn

7 1. actor, 2. director, 3. hairdresser, 4. waiter, 5. singer, 6. doctor, 7. football player

8 1. forgotten, 2. been, 3. won, 4. made

9 ↓ 1. vet, 3. grandma, 5. forgotten, 7. ever, 8. young
→ 2. embarrassed, 4. nervous, 6. yet

10 1. 2 p.m., 2. 8 a.m., 3. 11:59 a.m., 4. 10:15 p.m.

11 1. ticket, 2. sofa, 3. theatre, 4. world

12 1. remember, 2. panic, 3. believe, 4. Come out, 5. act

13 1. head, 2. ear, 3. nose, 4. mouth, 5. eye, 6. stomach, 7. arm, 8. leg, 9. foot

14 ache, sore, hurt, headache, tablets, ill

● 15 a) washing up, it, floor, cake, table, bottle bank, shopping, bottles, rubbish
b) done / washing up, taken / rubbish, made / cake, swept / floor, done / shopping, taken bottles / bottle bank, laid / table, eaten / it

● 16 1. nurse, 2. lorry driver, 3. builder, 4. shop assistant, 5. chef, 6. vet

Unit 3

1 city, boat trip, sights, big wheel, built, buildings, clock tower, royal, ago, prison, restaurant

2 1. even, 2. pretty, 3. fire, 4. expensive, 5. dome, 6. visitor

3 1. church – Kirche, 2. castle – Burg, 3. stadium – Stadion, 4. market – Markt, 5. bridge – Brücke, 6. taxi – Taxi, 7. bell – Glocke

4 1. one / a hundred and one, 2. five hundred and eighty-two, 3. three hundred and thirty-four, 4. three thousand and twenty-one, 5. nine thousand, two hundred and nineteen

5 1. London Eye: Height, weighs, tonnes, 2. Big Ben: high, bell, 3. St Paul's Cathedral: built, dome

6 1. office, 2. TV studio, 3. visitor, 4. sunbathe, 5. pretty, 6. fact

7 top, suits, isn't it, look for, size, shop assistant, these

8 1. dry – wet, trocken – nass, 2. small – big, klein – groß, 3. long – short, lang – kurz, 4. low – high, niedrig – hoch, 5. cheap – expensive, billig – teuer, 6. young – old, jung – alt, 7. grey – colourful, grau – bunt

9 ↓ 1. passenger, 2. sunglasses, 4. real, 5. price
→ 3. airport, 6. fly, 7. bargain, 8. each, 9. stickers

● 10 1. mosque, 2. lake, 3. monument, 4. square, 5. floor

● 11 1. loose, 2. unfashionable, 3. plain, 4. uncomfortable

● 12 1. lake, 2. square, 3. rent, 4. monument

● 13 1. nurse, 2. cannon, 3. cannon balls, 4. roof, 5. fire engine, 6. carpenter, 7. tools

● 14 1. boss, 2. across, 3. part, 4. as, 5. drama, 6. when

Unit 4

1 1. pie, 2. dumpling, 3. potato salad, 4. bread, 5. chicken, 6. pasta / spaghetti, 7. pork / ham, 8. rice, 9. sausage(s), 10. pasty, 11. salad, 12. vegetables, 13. potato(es), 14. cabbage, 15. carrot(s), 16. onion

2 grandma, Jamaican, spices, sort, delicious, coconut

3 1. choose, chose, chosen – auswählen, 2. spend, spent, spent – ausgeben, 3. fly, flew, flown – fliegen, 4. pay, paid, paid – bezahlen

4 1. starter, 2. main course, 3. dessert

5 1. packed lunch, 2. mashed potatoes, 3. apple crumble 4. pasta bake

6 usually, mashed potatoes, allergic, spent, payment, desserts

7 1. news, 2. many, 3. meal, 4. fried

8 → 2. soup, 4. strawberry, 7. tomato, 9. pudding
↓ 1. custard, 2. spaghetti, 3. garlic, 5. beef, 6. ham, 8. onion

9 1. cup, 2. glass, 3. plate, 4. fork, 5. knife, 6. spoon

10 2. plantain – Kochbanane, 3. wrap – Wrap, 4. napkin – Serviette, 5. combination – Kombination, 6. menu – Speisekarte, 7. thirsty – durstig, 8. order – bestellen

11 1. teen, 2. watch, 3. recipe, 4. chef, 5. judge, 6. kid, 7. piece, 8. milk

12 1. cook, 2. become, 3. prefer, 4. add

13 1. e), 2. d), 3. c), 4. a), 5. b)

14 1. good, 2. delicious, 3. pretty, 4. brilliant, 5. great, 6. lovely, 7. beautiful, 8. fantastic

15 Indian, takeaway, flyer, order, recipe, dishes

● 16 1. apple crumble, 2. tray, 3. lemon, 4. pancake, 5. mustard, 6. lamb, 7. spring roll, 8. lasagne, 9. cheesecake, 10. teaspoon; MAYONNAISE

● 17 1. straw, 2. bowl, 3. moussaka, 4. toothpick

● 18 1. chef, 2. college, 3. mine, 4. form, 5. working

● 19 1. b), 2. c), 3. a)

● 20 1. ingredient – Zutat, 2. lovely – schön, 3. magic – Zauberei, 4. second – Sekunde, 5. stir – umrühren

Unit 5

1 Hi Mike, Where are you? We are watching a great football match. Laugh out loud! We're losing. Talk to you later. See you tomorrow. Tina

2 1. gamer, 2. Good morning., 3. difficult, 4. treasure, 5. fantasy, 6. laugh, 7. kiss, 8. text message

3 1. c), 2. d), 3. a), 4. e), 5. b)

4 1. try on, 2. hang around, ride my bike, 3. on the bus, 4. has got, 5. wait for

5 1. laugh, 2. travel, 3. stand, 4. chat, 5. rap, 6. wave, 7. call

6 1. hang, hung, hung – hängen, 2. ride, rode, ridden – reiten, 3. stand, stood, stood – stehen, 4. swim, swam, swum – schwimmen

7 1. moment, 2. while, 3. clever

8 → 2. laugh, 6. hard, 7. ski, 8. test, 11. dream, 12. mile
↓ 1. online, 3. head, 4 rest, 5. children, 9. swim, 10. rap

9 What about you, at last, I don't think so, I disagree

10 1. children, 2. jacket, 3. roller coaster, 4. gamer, 5. wall, 6. lettuce

● 11 download, videos, comment, software, save, file, copy, paste

● 12 1. get dressed, 2. repair, 3. paint, 4. upload, 5. fit, 6. agree

Unit 6

1 1. Cornish, 2. soon, 3. smugglers, 4. away, 5. guys, 6. leave, 7. miss, 8. the best; GREENWICH

2 1. plan, 2. three more days, 3. leaving, 4. jealous, 5. when, 6. Congratulations

3 1. camping, 2. beach combing, 3. umbrella, 4. jewellery, 5. play table tennis, 6. look after

4 1. Is something wrong? 2. This is my farewell speech. 3. Hmm. I love your scones! 4. Don't eat too much! 5. Would you like a bit?

5 1. agree, agreed, agreed – zustimmen, 2. leave, left, left – verlassen, 3. miss, missed, missed – vermissen, 4. stand, stood, stood – stehen, 5. understand, understood, understood – verstehen, 6. wave, waved, waved – winken

6 a) clever, silly, jealous, thirsty, fresh, hard
b) 1. Al – clever, 2. Rob – silly, 3. Mike – jealous, 4. Mary – thirsty, 5. apples – fresh, 6. it – hard

7 1. all / everyone, 2. maybe, 3. forever

8 1. b), 2. a), 3. d), 4. c)

9 1. cave – Höhle, 2. flag – Fahne, 3. harbour – Hafen, 4. ghost – Geist, 5. mountain – Berg, 6. sunglasses – Sonnenbrille

10 1. flag, 2. ghost, 3. creak, 4. against, 5. silly, 6. before, 7. scone, 8. secret, 9. strange, 10. umbrella, 11. inside, 12. scare

● 11 tent, combing, waves, woods, streams, explore, school, goodbye, pack, address, feel, forever

● 12 1. rock, 2. funny / strange, 3. now, 4. address, 5. only, 6. sell

Arbeitsanweisungen mit Operatoren

Complete the sentences • the dialogue • the text • the table.
Vervollständige die Sätze • den Dialog • den Text • die Tabelle.

Describe the people • the picture(s).
Beschreibe die Menschen • das Bild/die Bilder.

Find the words • the verbs • the pairs • the phrases • the activities and write them (down) • write them in the right order.
Finde die Wörter • die Verben • die Paare • die Satzteile • die Aktivitäten und schreibe sie auf • schreibe sie in der richtigen Reihenfolge.

Find the wrong word.
Finde das falsche Wort.

Look at the pictures.
Schau dir die Bilder an.

Match the words • the (sentence) parts.
Ordne die Wörter • die Satzteile zu.

Make sentences.
Bilde Sätze.

Put in the right verb • the right form of the verb.
Setze das richtige Verb • die richtige Form des Verbs ein.

Write the (missing) words • numbers • the phrases in English.
Schreibe die (fehlenden) Wörter • Nummern • Satzteile auf Englisch auf.

Write the right word • the opposites.
Schreibe das richtige Wort • die Gegenteile auf.

Write the words next to the German.
Schreibe die Wörter neben das Deutsche.

Notizen

Notizen